W9-DDS-359

# The
# Bill of Rights

## by Michael Burgan

Content Adviser: Professor Sherry L. Field,
Department of Social Science Education, College of Education,
The University of Georgia

XAIP3760201856

Reading Adviser: Dr. Linda D. Labbo,
Department of Reading Education, College of Education,
The University of Georgia

**COMPASS POINT BOOKS**
Minneapolis, Minnesota

Compass Point Books
3109 West 50th Street, #115
Minneapolis, MN 55410

Visit Compass Point Books on the Internet at *www.compasspointbooks.com* or e-mail your request
to *custserv@compasspointbooks.com*

Photographs ©: Hulton Getty/Archive Photos, cover, 4, 5, 7, 9, 16, 17, 32; North Wind Picture
Archives: 6, 8, 11, 12, 13, 14, 18, 21, 23, 27, 30, 37, 38, 40; Archive Photos, 10, 24; Stock
Montage, 15, 20, 26; Library of Congress, 28; Kevin Fleming/Corbis, 33; Reuters/Mike
Theiler/Archive Photos, 35; XNR Productions, Inc., 36.

Editors: E. Russell Primm, Emily J. Dolbear, and Deborah Cannarella
Photo Researcher: Svetlana Zhurkina
Photo Selector: Linda S. Koutris
Designer: Bradfordesign, Inc.
Cartographer: XNR Productions, Inc.

**Library of Congress Cataloging-in-Publication Data**

Burgan, Michael.
    The Bill of Rights / by Michael Burgan.
        p. cm. — (We the people)
    Includes bibliographical references and index.
    ISBN 0-7565-0151-2 (hardcover)
    ISBN 0-7565-0932-7 (paperback)
        1. United States. Constitution. 1st–10th Amendments—Juvenile literature. 2. Civil rights—
United States—History—Juvenile literature. 3. Constitutional amendments—United States—
History—Juvenile literature. I. Title. II. We the people (Compass Point Books)
    KF4750 .B87 2002
    342.73'085—dc21                                    2001001570

# TABLE OF CONTENTS

# READY FOR A BATTLE

During the first few months of 1789, snow and ice gripped much of the United States. The harsh weather made it hard for many Americans to work and travel—and to vote in the first elections held under the new **Constitution**. By spring, some members of the new House of Representatives still had to battle the weather as they set off to take part in the government.

*Madison and others wrote the U.S. Constitution at Independence Hall in Philadelphia.*

James Madison, a representative from Virginia, spent almost two weeks traveling to New York City, the temporary capital of the nation. Wintry weather was not Madison's biggest problem as he prepared to enter the House. Almost two years earlier, Madison had helped write the Constitution. This is the document that describes basic U.S. laws, including the rights of the people and the powers of the government. Madison had pushed for its acceptance across the country. Now, the Constitution was under attack.

Before the creation of the Constitution, the thirteen American states sometimes acted like separate countries. The federal, or national, government was weak. People such as Madison wanted a new, stronger government for the United States,

*James Madison*

5

*Patrick Henry*

and the Constitution created that government. Madison and other supporters of the Constitution were called Federalists.

People who opposed the Constitution were known as Anti-Federalists. Most of them thought the Constitution gave the federal government too much power. The Anti-Federalists feared that state governments and individual citizens would lose some of their rights. Patrick Henry, also of Virginia, was a leading Anti-Federalist. During the American Revolution (1775–1783), he became famous for his stirring cry, "Give me liberty or give me death."

Madison knew that Patrick Henry and others wanted to make a number of **amendments,** or changes, to the Constitution. The Anti-Federalists hoped to weaken federal control over the states. Others demanded a bill of rights—a list of freedoms that the government could not take away from its citizens. Now, Madison had to try to preserve the new government he had worked so hard to create. He knew that drafting a bill of rights was one way to do this.

*The Bill of Rights*

# CREATING A NEW GOVERNMENT

The split between Federalists and Anti-Federalists began in 1787 at the Constitutional **Convention**. Political leaders from all thirteen states except Rhode Island gathered in Philadelphia, Pennsylvania, to discuss a new U.S. government. This convention lasted almost four months. Madison led the call for a government with "national authority," which the old government lacked.

*The Constitutional Convention of 1787 lasted almost four months.*

*Congress was one of the three branches of government Madison proposed.*

Madison proposed a government with three parts, or branches. The legislature—or Congress—would have two separate houses, with representatives sent by the states. This branch would make laws. The executive branch would carry out these laws. "President" was later chosen as the title for the head of the executive branch. The third branch was the judiciary, or court system. Its judges would make sure the laws were carried out fairly.

The **delegates** at the convention debated the details

9

*George Mason*

of Madison's plan. In the end, they accepted most of what he proposed. Some delegates, however, wanted a bill of rights. George Mason had written a bill of rights for the state constitution in Virginia. Other states, including Pennsylvania, Maryland, and Delaware, also had a bill of rights in their constitutions. Mason said that a national bill of rights would "give great quiet" to Americans who feared losing their freedoms. Elbridge Gerry of Massachusetts also supported a bill of rights, but the convention rejected his call to discuss the idea.

On September 17, 1787, thirty-nine delegates signed the Constitution. They represented eleven of the thirteen states. (Alexander Hamilton of New York, a leading

*The signers of the U.S. Constitution*

Federalist, also signed, but he was not officially representing his state). Before he signed, Pennsylvania's Benjamin Franklin said, "Thus I consent . . . to this Constitution because I expect no better, and because I am not sure, it is not the best." Other Americans, however, were not so sure the new government was the best. The Anti-Federalists hoped to stop the Constitution from becoming the law of the land.

# THE FIGHT TO RATIFY

The debate over the Constitution then moved from Philadelphia to the individual states. Nine of the thirteen states had to **ratify**, or approve, the document. Within each state, Federalists and Anti-Federalists argued over the Constitution. Anti-Federalists hoped to kill the document altogether or at least improve it with a bill of rights.

*The debate over ratification of the Constitution moved to the individual states after it was signed in Philadelphia.*

Federalists did not think the Constitution needed to spell out the protection of certain rights. Some people called for the right to freedom of the press. However, Federalist James Wilson argued that the Constitution did not give Congress any power over the press so there was no need to specify the freedom of the press. "It would have been . . . absurd," Wilson said, "to have [declared to] a federal body of our own creation, that we should enjoy those privileges of which we are not [deprived]."

*James Wilson*

The Anti-Federalists, however, did not accept this or similar arguments. They feared that without a guarantee of specific rights, individuals or small groups of people would lose their freedoms. A bill of rights would protect these minorities against the majority, or larger number, of citizens.

*Groups on both sides of the issue held discussions all around the country.*

Despite the protests against the Constitution, several states quickly ratified it. Delaware was the first, on December 7, 1787. Pennsylvania, New Jersey, Georgia, and Connecticut soon followed. In most of these states, Federalists dominated the conventions where the Constitution was discussed.

14

The battle to ratify was harder in Massachusetts. There, Elbridge Gerry was one of several important political leaders who opposed the Constitution. Massachusetts eventually accepted the document, but the Anti-Federalists won a small victory. They sent along nine proposed amendments for Congress to consider.

*Elbridge Gerry*

After Massachusetts, every state except Maryland called for amendments, a bill of rights, or a second Constitutional Convention. The most important debates over these proposed changes came in New York and Virginia. In New York, Alexander

15

Hamilton led the Federalists. He, along with Madison and John Jay, wrote a series of articles defending the Constitution. These articles were later collected into a book called *The Federalist*.

Hamilton believed that a bill of rights was necessary only to protect citizens from the power of kings and that democratic government did not need one. "The truth is," Hamilton wrote, "that the Constitution is itself in every rational sense, and to every useful purpose a BILL OF RIGHTS." Hamilton was able

*John Jay*

*Alexander Hamilton*

*Patrick Henry argued his cause before the Virginia Assembly.*

to convince the New York convention to accept the
Constitution, but the state added thirty-two proposed
amendments.

Federalist forces in Virginia included Madison and
George Washington. Opposing them were such leaders as

18

Patrick Henry and George Mason. Henry spoke passionately against the Constitution. He said the new government could take away some of the rights protected by Virginia's own Declaration of Rights. "This Constitution is said to have beautiful features," Henry said. "But when I come to examine these features, Sir, they appear to me horridly frightful."

Virginia could have been the ninth state to ratify the Constitution, and its vote would have put a new government into place. However, Henry did not want that honor for Virginia. He said the other eight states already had "heart burnings and animosity" over their decision to ratify. New Hampshire became the ninth state to ratify, on June 21, 1788, but the Federalists knew it was important for Virginia to accept the new government. The state was one of the nation's largest and wealthiest. In a close vote, Virginia finally ratified the Constitution, but it also called for a bill of rights. The issue of protecting individual rights was not yet over.

# MADISON CHANGES HIS MIND

One of America's political leaders had not played a part in drafting the Constitution. Thomas Jefferson, one of the most brilliant thinkers of his day, had written the Declaration of Independence and the Virginia law that protected religious freedom. During the debates over the Constitution, Jefferson was in Paris

*Thomas Jefferson*

where he served as America's ambassador to France. But he still had an impact on the issue of a bill of rights.

*James Madison was affected by Jefferson's ideas.*

Late in 1787, Madison wrote a letter to Jefferson describing the Constitution. Jefferson wrote back with his comments. He thought the document needed a bill of rights that "provided clearly . . . for freedom of religion, freedom of the press, protection against standing armies . . ." and other rights. Jefferson added that a bill of rights was "what the people are entitled to against every government on earth."

Madison was not totally against a bill of rights, but he did not want to give in to the Anti-Federalists. Madison also thought that a government might need to limit some rights during a crisis. By June 1788, however, Madison was ready to give in. He realized the Anti-Federalists in Virginia would not support the Constitution without a bill of rights.

Jefferson also helped convince Madison to accept a bill of rights. He wrote to Madison in March 1789 and described again why a bill of rights was important. The judiciary could use it to protect the rights of minorities. If Congress passed a law that denied freedoms, for example, the courts could then use the bill of rights to overturn that law.

By this time, Madison had been elected to the House of Representatives. He had promised the voters in Virginia that he would work for a bill of rights. Another leading Virginian also wanted a bill of rights. In April 1789,

*George Washington was sworn in as the nation's first president in April 1789.*

George Washington was sworn in as the first president of the United States. He thought Congress should amend the Constitution to guarantee basic rights, but without destroying "the benefits of a united and effective government."

# BACK TO WORK

Madison then agreed to draft a bill of rights. He studied state constitutions for ideas. He also considered the suggestions made by the states during the debates over the Constitution. In June 1789, Madison presented his proposed amendments to the House of Representatives. Madison said that a bill of rights was good for the "tranquility of the public mind, and the stability of the government."

*Madison's amendments to the Constitution were presented to Congress in June 1789.*

24

Most Federalists still did not want a bill of rights. They believed most Americans liked the Constitution as it was. Why else had the states ratified it so quickly? The Federalists also thought Congress had more important issues to handle. The lawmakers still had to work out the details of running the new national government.

Surprisingly, many Anti-Federalists also opposed Madison's plan. They did not really want to add a bill of rights to the Constitution. Instead, they hoped to call a second Constitutional Convention for the nation. There, the Anti-Federalists planned to create a new federal government with less control over the states. The Anti-Federalists lacked the power to put their plan into action, however.

For six weeks, Congress refused to consider Madison's amendments. Finally, in August, the House began to discuss them. Roger Sherman of Connecticut quickly asked for one change in Madison's plan. Madison wanted the amendments inserted into the Constitution at

*Roger Sherman*

various places. Sherman insisted that they be added at the end. He and others did not want future Americans to think the amendments had been part of the original Constitution. Congress accepted Sherman's plan.

Madison's amendments included freedom of the press, the freedom to practice any religion, and the right to own guns. He proposed that anyone charged with a crime receive a fast, fair trial with a jury. One amendment also said that any powers not given to the federal government in the Constitution belonged to the states.

*Freedom of religion was one of the rights included in Madison's amendments.*

The House debated Madison's amendments through August. At the end of the month, it sent seventeen amendments to the Senate for its reaction. The senators combined some of the amendments and dropped one, leaving twelve.

**27**

*William Grayson*

Then Senate and House members met to discuss them. Finally, on September 24, 1789, the House agreed to the final wording of the amendments and the Senate did the same the next day.

Not everyone was pleased with the final result. Senator William Grayson of Virginia wrote that the amendments "are good for nothing, and I believe, as many others do, that they will do more harm than benefit." But George Mason of Virginia said he "received much satisfaction from the amendments."

28

# RATIFY—AGAIN

The twelve amendments were sent out to each state to ratify. New Jersey was the first, in November 1789. Soon nine states had approved almost all of the amendments. By mid-1791, only four states had not approved the Bill of Rights. By this time, Vermont had entered the Union as the fourteenth state so now eleven states had to approve the Bill of Rights before it could become law. Vermont was the tenth, and people wondered which state would be number eleven.

Once again, Virginia's vote was considered crucial. Anti-Federalist forces there still hoped to block the Bill of Rights and call for a new Constitutional Convention. But many important Virginians backed the amendments. Thomas Jefferson had returned from France and was now U.S. secretary of state. He supported ratification in his home state. Finally, on December 15, 1791, Virginia ratified the Bill of Rights. (The other remaining states—

*Jefferson, who returned from France in 1789, supported the amendments.*

Georgia, Connecticut, and Massachusetts—did not ratify the Bill of Rights until 1939.)

The final list of rights included ten of the twelve originally sent out by Congress. The states rejected the first two amendments. One dealt with the number of representatives in the House and the other concerned future pay raises for Congress. Without these two amendments, the Bill of Rights began with the guarantees of free speech, a free press, and freedom of religion.

# AFTER THE BILL OF RIGHTS

With the Bill of Rights in place, more Americans now supported the Constitution. The remaining Anti-Federalists lost whatever influence they once had. But the conflict between people who supported a strong national government and those who favored states' rights

*The issue of slavery, and eventually voting rights for African-Americans, would not be settled by the Constitution until after the Civil War.*

did not end. During the nineteenth century, that issue was at the heart of the conflict over slavery. People who opposed slavery wanted to use the power of the federal government to end it. Supporters of slavery said each state had the right to make slavery legal.

The slavery issue was settled after the Civil War (1861–1865). New amendments to the Constitution made

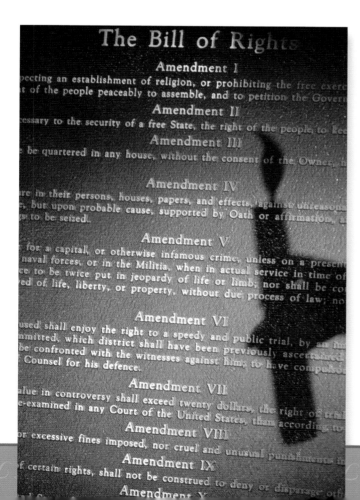

*The Bill of Rights is inscribed on a bronze plaque in front of the Wilmington, Delaware, federal building.*

33

slavery illegal and gave African-Americans legal rights. Before that time, slaves had no legal rights under the Constitution. Even freed slaves often lacked the protection of the Bill of Rights.

The Fourteenth Amendment was particularly important. This amendment limited the power of states to deny the freedom of individuals. With the Fourteenth Amendment, the Bill of Rights now applied to state governments as well. In the words of one legal scholar, the "extension of the Bill of Rights against the states has, in general, dramatically strengthened the Bill." In his original bill of rights, Madison had actually proposed limits on a state's ability to restrict the freedoms of speech, religion, and conscience. The Senate, however, removed this amendment, regarding the Bill of Rights as limiting only the federal government.

Madison is remembered as the Father of the Bill of Rights. Despite his own doubts about a bill of rights, he worked hard to make it a reality. Today, the U.S. Supreme

34

*The Bill of Rights is central to many of today's U.S. Supreme Court rulings.*

Court still uses the Bill of Rights —the first ten amendments of the Constitution—to determine whether laws are just. People sometimes disagree on how the Court uses the Bill of Rights or the rest of the Constitution. But most Americans agree that the Bill of Rights is a great protector of their freedoms.

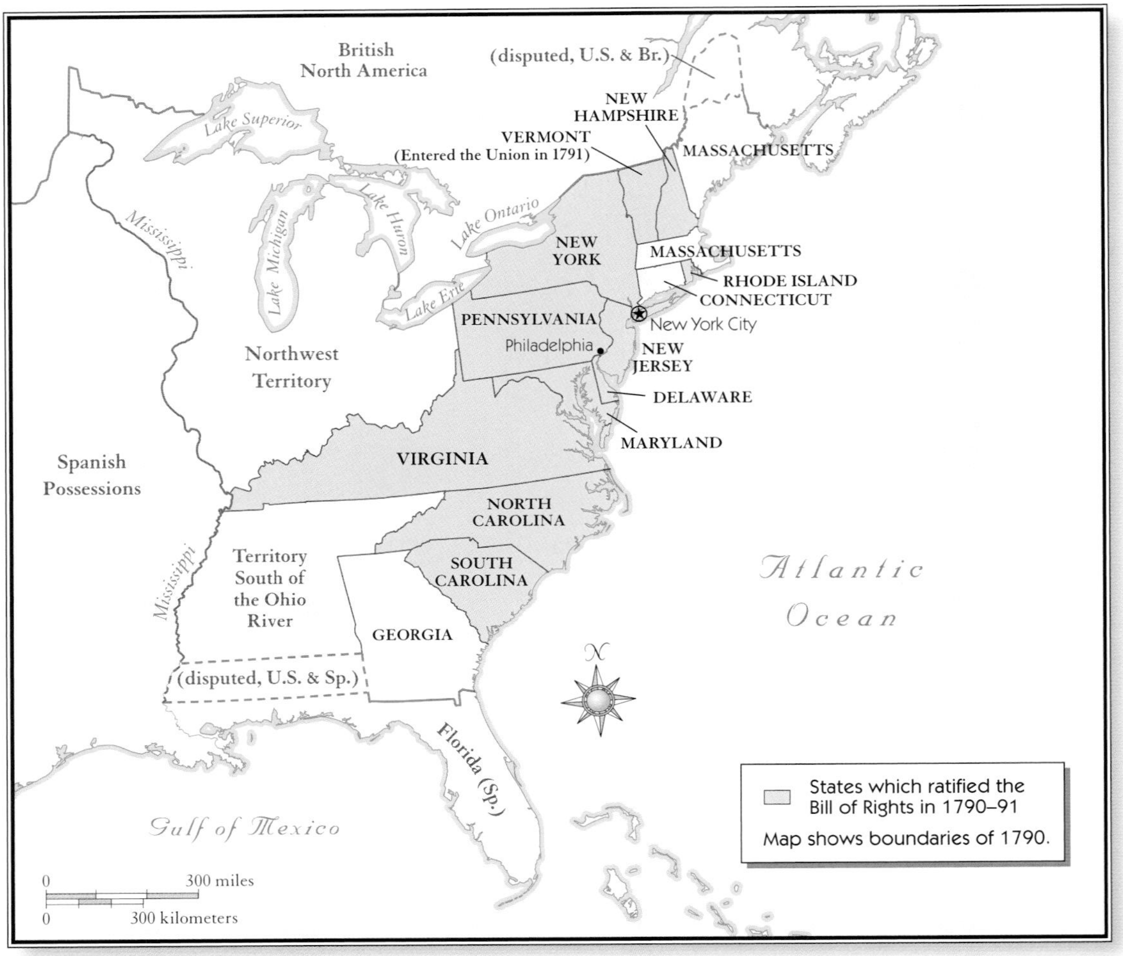
British North America
(disputed, U.S. & Br.)
NEW HAMPSHIRE
VERMONT (Entered the Union in 1791)
MASSACHUSETTS
Lake Superior
Lake Huron
Lake Michigan
Lake Ontario
Lake Erie
Mississippi
NEW YORK
MASSACHUSETTS
RHODE ISLAND
CONNECTICUT
PENNSYLVANIA
New York City
Philadelphia
NEW JERSEY
DELAWARE
MARYLAND
Northwest Territory
Spanish Possessions
VIRGINIA
NORTH CAROLINA
SOUTH CAROLINA
Territory South of the Ohio River
GEORGIA
(disputed, U.S. & Sp.)
Atlantic Ocean
N
Florida (Sp.)
Gulf of Mexico
0 300 miles
0 300 kilometers
States which ratified the Bill of Rights in 1790–91
Map shows boundaries of 1790.

*Map showing the states which ratified the Bill of Rights in 1790-1791.*

# THE BILL OF RIGHTS

The First Ten Amendments to the U.S. Constitution

**First Amendment**

Congress shall make no law respecting an establishment of religion, or prohibiting the free exercise thereof; or abridging the freedom of speech, or of the press; or the right of the people peaceably to assemble, and to petition the government for a redress of grievances.

*Freedom of the press is guaranteed by the First Amendment.*

*Many believe that the right to own guns is protected by the Second Amendment.*

## Second Amendment

A well regulated militia, being necessary to the security of a free state, the right of the people to keep and bear arms, shall not be infringed.

### Third Amendment

No soldier shall, in time of peace, be quartered in any house without the consent of the owner; nor in time of war but in a manner to be prescribed by law.

### Fourth Amendment

The right of the people to be secure in their persons, houses, papers, and effects, against unreasonable searches and seizures, shall not be violated, and no warrants shall issue but upon probable cause, supported by oath or affirmation, and particularly describing the place to be searched, and the persons or things to be seized.

### Fifth Amendment

No person shall be held to answer for a capital, or otherwise infamous crime, unless on a presentment or indictment of a grand jury, except in cases arising in the land or naval forces, or in the militia, when in actual service in time of war or public danger; nor shall any person be subject for the same offence to be twice put in jeopardy of life or limb; nor shall be compelled in any criminal case to be a witness

*The right to trial with a jury of one's peers is guaranteed in the Sixth Amendment.*

against himself, nor be deprived of life, liberty, or property, without due process of law; nor shall private property be taken for public use, without just compensation.

### Sixth Amendment

In all criminal prosecutions, the accused shall enjoy the right to a speedy and public trial, by an impartial jury of the state and district wherein the crime shall have been committed, which district shall have been previously ascertained by law, and to be informed of the nature and cause of the accusation; to be confronted with the witness-es against him; to have compulsory process for obtaining witnesses in his favor, and to have the assistance of counsel for his defense.

### Seventh Amendment

In suits at common law, where the value in controversy shall exceed twenty dollars, the right of trial by jury shall be preserved, and no fact tried by a jury, shall be otherwise reexamined in any court of the United States, than according to the rules of the common law.

### Eighth Amendment

Excessive bail shall not be required, nor excessive fines imposed, nor cruel and unusual punishments inflicted.

### Ninth Amendment

The enumeration in the Constitution, of certain rights, shall not be construed to deny or disparage others retained by the people.

### Tenth Amendment

The powers not delegated to the United States by the Constitution, nor prohibited by it to the states, are reserved to the states respectively, or to the people.

# GLOSSARY

**amendments**—changes made to a law or legal document

**Constitution**—the document that describes the basic laws and principles by which the nation is governed

**convention**—a meeting of people who have the same interests

**delegates**—people who represent a larger group of people at a meeting

**ratify**—to agree to; to approve officially

# DID YOU KNOW?

- The Virginia Declaration of Rights written in June 1776 served as a model for the United States Bill of Rights.

- James Madison became the fourth president of the United States in 1809. He is known as the Father of the Constitution.

- The Bill of Rights is the most extensive government document outlining personal liberties in the world today.

- Roger Sherman was the only person to sign all four of these great documents: Articles of Association (1774), the Declaration of Independence (1776), the the Articles of Confederation (1777), and the U.S. Constitution (1787).

# IMPORTANT DATES

## Timeline

**1787**
May: Constitutional Convention opens in Philadelphia, Pennsylvania; September: Delegates approve final draft of the new Constitution; December: Delaware becomes first state to ratify the Constitution.

**1788**
June: New Hampshire becomes the ninth state to ratify the Constitution, putting the new government in place.

**1789**
April: Congress officially meets for the first time; George Washington is sworn in as first U.S. president; June: Madison introduces his proposed amendments to the Constitution; September: Congress sends twelve amendments to the states for their approval; November: New Jersey becomes the first state to ratify the amendments.

**1791**
December: The first ten amendments to the Constitution take effect.

# IMPORTANT PEOPLE

## ALEXANDER HAMILTON

**(1755–1804),** *member of the Constitutional Convention and co-author of* The Federalist, *with John Jay and James Madison*

## PATRICK HENRY

**(1736–1799),** *American Revolutionary hero, orator, and leader for adoption of the Bill of Rights*

## JOHN JAY

**(1745–1829)**, *co-author of* The Federalist

## JAMES MADISON

**(1751–1836)**, *fourth president of the United States*

## GEORGE MASON

**(1725–1792),** *statesman who opposed the Constitution and was instrumental in adoption of the Bill of Rights*

## GEORGE WASHINGTON

**(1732–1799)**, *first president of the United States*

# WANT TO KNOW MORE?

## At the Library

Bjornlund, Lydia D. *The Constitution and the Founding of America.*
   San Diego: Lucent Books, 2000.

Grote, JoAnn A. *Patrick Henry.* Philadelphia: Chelsea House, 1999.

Malone, Mary. *James Madison.* Springfield, N.J.: Enslow Publishers, 1997.

Monk, Linda R. *The Bill of Rights: A User's Guide.* Alexandria, VA: Close
   Up Publishing, 1995.

Quiri, Patricia Ryon. *The Bill of Rights.* Danbury, Conn.: Children's Press,
   1998.

Sobel, Syd. *How the U.S. Government Works.* Hauppauge, N.Y.: Barron's
   Juvenile, 1999.

## On the Web

For more information on the *Bill of Rights,* use

FactHound to track down Web sites related to this book.

1. Go to *www.compasspointbooks.com/facthound*

2. Type in this book ID: 0756501512

3. Click on the *Fetch It* button.

Your trusty FactHound will fetch the best Web sites for you!

## Through the Mail

**The National Archives and Records Administration**

700 Pennsylvania Avenue, N.W.

Washington, D.C. 20408

To learn more about the historical documents related to the founding of the United States

## On the Road

**Montpelier**

11407 Constitution Highway

Montpelier Station, VA 22957

540/672-2728

To tour the home of James Madison

# Index

## About the Author

Michael Burgan is a freelance writer for children and adults. A history graduate of the University of Connecticut, he has written more than thirty fiction and nonfiction children's books for various publishers. For adult audiences, he has written news articles, essays, and plays. Michael Burgan is a recipient of an Edpress Award and belongs to the Society of Children's Book Writers and Illustrators.